CASTLES OF BRITAIN   2 SCOTLAND

CONTENTS

Cover photograph: Edinburgh Castle

Frontispiece: Dunnottar Castle

Acknowledgements

The publishers acknowledge the following for permission to use photographs: Aerofilms Ltd., British Travel and Holidays Association, Central Office of Information, Ministry of Public Buildings and Works, Edinburgh, Radio Times Hulton Picture Library, Scottish National Buildings Record.

Authors Note

In a work of this kind it is obviously impossible to include all the notable castles of Scotland, and while the author has attempted to include examples of the different types, the selection is a purely personal one. She apologises, therefore, to those readers who may find that their most cherished castle has been omitted.

Castles of Britain

2 Scotland

by
Muriel Hammond

LONDON

IAN ALLAN

Introduction

In England and Wales the castle was the badge of the defeated country, the Norman conqueror introducing the castle into England, and Edward I consolidating his position in the Principality by its erection. The Scottish castle seems also to have been introduced by the Norman, but he came by invitation and acquired his lands by marriage and gift rather than by force of arms.

The earliest fortifications, as in England, were of earth and wood, but more typical of the north was the Broch (or Burgh), of which the most famous example is the Broch of Mousa, in Shetland. The Broch consisted of an immensely thick round wall built of dry stone, without mortar or cement, enclosing an open court. It was entered by a low narrow passage, which was probably blocked in time of trouble with a stone slab. The Broch appears to have been built solely for defence, and it has been suggested that it served the Celts as a refuge from the slave-raiders of imperial Rome.

Broch of Mousa

For a long time it was thought that there were no Norman castles of the traditional motte-and-bailey type in Scotland, but more recent research tends to the belief that they vanished during the Wars of Independence, during the late thirteenth and fourteenth centuries, or were rebuilt and altered in style. Certainly there are a number of mounds which could well have been mottes, the Peel of Lumphanan, the Doune of Invernochty and the Bass of Inverurie, to name only a few of the better known examples, though there is a possibility that these were primitive ceremonial mounds, from which laws and judgments were delivered.

Lack of reliable contemporary documents makes the task of dating the older Scottish castles difficult if not impossible. Few kingdoms can have had a more troubled history. Under Malcolm Canmore, David I, Alexander II and Alexander III, Scotland enjoyed a relatively stable government, with peace at home and abroad, but from the death of Alexander III in 1286 until the union of the crowns of England and Scotland in 1603, there was little but war and destruction. Small wonder, therefore, that an element of guesswork enters into the dating of castles, which, from their very nature, were particularly vulnerable in wartime, subject to constant attack and change of ownership, with resultant alteration in structure.

Cobbie Row's Castle

One of the oldest castles which can be dated with any degree of accuracy is Cobbie Row's Castle on the island of Wyre in the Orkneys, though strictly this is Norse and not Scottish, the Orkneys belonging to Norway until 1468. The *Orkneyinga Saga* relates the building in about 1145 of a stone castle by the Norseman, Kolbein Hruga, and all the evidence points to this being Cobbie Row's. Only a few feet of the walls remain, but enough to show that the castle consisted of a small tower, about 15 feet square internally, with walls 5 feet thick, the whole surrounded by a round ditch. In other words, a Norman keep of traditional design, but built by a Norseman and not one of his Latinised brethren from Normandy. A similar example almost certainly of Norse origin is the castle of Sween in Argyllshire (*see page 19*).

The thirteenth century was the era of Scotland's finest castle-building. Under Alexander II and III the kingdom enjoyed a period of great prosperity, when both secular and ecclesiastical architecture of a high standard rose apace. To this period belong such remarkable castles as Bothwell, Dirleton and Kildrummy, castles which can rival those of Edward I in Wales. Some were, in fact, strengthened and enlarged by Edward's architects after being captured by the English in the Wars of Independence, but they were already fortresses of considerable importance. For the most part, these were all castles of enceinte, with a curtain wall surrounding a bailey, and one tower of greater strength than the rest to serve as a keep. Later came the Edwardian idea of the keep-gatehouse, thrusting aggressively forward from the curtain, built for offence rather than defence. Both Kildrummy and Caerlaverock acquired such gatehouses, and it is more than likely that Bothwell had one in the now vanished north curtain.

The golden age ended in 1286 with the death of Alexander III, who left as his sole heir his baby grand-daughter, Margaret the Maid of of Norway. On her death, in 1290, Edward I was called upon to mediate between the rival claimants to the throne and gave his support to John Baliol, who reigned for four uncertain years, until his dispossession in 1296. Edward was now more concerned about the Crown, and there followed a half-century of bitter, desperate fighting. This was the age of the great patriots, of Wallace, of Bruce (later Robert I), Sir Andrew Moray and women as gallant as their men; Dame Christian Bruce who held Kildrummy, and " Black " Agnes Randolph, who defended Dunbar.

With his victory at Bannockburn, Bruce secured a brief, uneasy peace for Scotland, but there was little building during his reign. On the the contrary, he was the pioneer of the " scorched earth " policy, which proved so successful in the defeat of Napoleon and other modern aggressors. Once a castle had been recovered from the English, Bruce and his supporters dismantled it, so that the invaders should have no foothold in the event of any future victories. Bruce did, however, erect Tarbert Castle, for the maintenance of order in the Highlands, and authorised the preservation of certain others.

These troubled times produced nothing more ambitious than the peel-tower. The derivation of the word is obscure, some authorities giving it as Latin *pila* (an arrow), and others as Latin *palus* (a stake, whence " palisade "). This type of fortification is typical of the Scottish

7

scene: based on the square Norman keep, it was still being built, with some modifications, as late as the seventeenth century, and at one time it was legislated that all landowners having property to the value of £100 or more should erect such a tower and enclose it with a barmkin or defensive wall.

In its simplest form, the tower-house, like the keep, consisted of a ground-floor store, possibly with a loft for servants, a great hall on the first floor, and the lord's private apartments above; entrance was generally at first-floor level, often by means of a ladder. The defences would consist of a crenellated parapet, sometimes machicolated, and often with small angle turrets or bartizans—these last are largely responsible for the faintly continental appearance of so many Scottish castles.

Life in a tower proving rather cramped, it became common to add an extra wing at one corner. This frequently contained the main stair (a somewhat wasteful arrangement), but could also accommodate a guardroom, kitchen and bedrooms. The rooms were usually lower than those in the main block, thereby enabling the builders to fit in an extra storey. The angle between the two towers—the re-entrant angle—provided a well-defended position for the entrance, which could now be brought down to ground-level without sacrificing security.

This type of building is known as L-plan. Two good examples are Craigmillar and Dunnotar, while at Glamis an L-plan tower lurks beneath the accretions of later years. A logical development from the L-plan was the Z-plan, constructed with a flanking tower at diagonally opposed corners. This provided still more accommodation, while adhering to the basic characteristics of the towerhouse, which, for all its inconvenience, provided maximum security at minimum cost. The flanking towers each covered two faces of the main block and were generally well supplied with gunloops, (Noltland, for example, has a superfluity) so that it would be a wily attacker indeed who could approach such a castle unobserved and unscathed. The flanking towers might be either square, as at Noltland and Glenbuchat, or round, as at Claypotts, while Midmar has one round and one square.

For the most part the defences of the Scottish castle were like those of the English; an embattled parapet, often machicolated, a portcullis and drawbridge, and perhaps a meurtière over the gate. More typically Scottish were the bartizan and the yett. This last was an iron gate formed of bars penetrating each other horizontally and vertically, the method of intersection being reversed in alternating panels. Hung within a wooden door, the yett proved so difficult to cope with that it was destroyed in most castles by order of the Privy Council in 1606. A few favoured lairds were exempted from this ruling, so yetts may still be studied at Doune, Glamis and Coxton.

The castle had a longer history in Scotland than in either England or

Wales. Doune, Tantallon and Ravenscraig are major castles of comparatively late date, and the tower-house was being built long after the Englishman had ceased even to fortify his manor. Artillery fortifications, either in the form of gun-ports or the more elaborate arrangements at Ravenscraig, are, accordingly, a fairly common feature of the Scottish castle.

Major sieges were conducted in the sixteenth century and the castle played an active military rôle in the religious wars of the seventeenth. After the Restoration in 1660, Scotland embarked at last upon a period of relative peace, with outbreaks of unrest under William III of England and two final explosions in 1715 and 1745. Castles like Edinburgh and Stirling saw some of the fighting of the Jacobite Rebellions, but by that time the methods of war had altered so completely that the military value of the castle was negligible. A few were dismantled after the collapse of the Rebellions; most were just allowed to fall into ruins and a small minority survive as museums and private residences.

THE SOVEREIGNS OF SCOTLAND, 1057-1603

Malcolm III (Canmore), 1057–93

Donald II, brother of Malcolm *and*
Edmund, son of Malcolm, 1093–94

Duncan II, son of Malcolm, 1094

Donald II *and*
Edmund (restored), 1094–97

Edgar, son of Malcolm, 1097–1107

Alexander I, son of Malcolm, 1107–24

David I, son of Malcolm, 1124–53

Malcolm IV, 1153–65

William I (the Lion), 1165–1214

Alexander II, 1214–49

Alexander III, 1249–86

Margaret (the Maid of Norway), 1286–90

Interregnum, 1290–92

John Baliol, 1292–96

Interregnum, 1296–1306

Robert I (the Bruce), 1306–29

David II, 1329–71

Robert II, 1371–89

Robert III, 1390–1406

James I, 1406–37

James II, 1437–60

James III, 1460–88

James IV, 1488–1513

James V, 1513–42

Mary, 1542–67

James VI (1603–25, James I of England), 1567–1625

Aberdeenshire

DRUM

In February 1323/24, the lands of Drum were conceded by Robert Bruce to his armour-bearer, William de Irwin, and the keep dates from about this time. It is a simple rectangular tower, about 53 by 40 feet in size and 70 feet high. The corners are rounded, right up to the top of the parapet, which has crenellations of the type more often to be seen on a curtain wall than on a tower. The drainage arrangements on the parapet-walk make it difficult to negotiate, so to counteract this, the the inner face of the wall has been niched, in order to provide an extra foothold.

The only projection on the outer walls of the keep is that formed by the latrine on the parapet-walk. Nor are there many openings. The ground floor has two ventilation slits only and was reached by a mural staircase from the first floor. Entrance to the keep was by way of a ladder or a timber stair leading to the common hall on the first floor. The lord's hall on the second floor has larger windows than the other rooms in the tower, with seats in the window recesses in the north and south walls. There is a good fireplace in the north wall and a latrine in the north-west angle.

In the early seventeenth century a pleasant manor house was built adjoining the keep, but the external structure of the tower remained virtually unaltered, so that, to this day, Drum is an almost perfect example of the small castle of the fourteenth century.

Glenbuchat Castle

GLENBUCHAT

Glenbuchat, situated about five miles from Kildrummy, is a fine example of the latest phase in Scottish military architecture. It is built on the Z-plan, with a square tower at the north-east and south-west angles of the central block, and is liberally provided with gun-loops, one of which is slanted so as to cover the entrance.

An inscription over the doorway, now illegible, commemorates the first owners:—

> Iohn Gordone, Helen Carnege, 1590
> No thing on Earth remanis bot faime.

The entrance, in the south-west tower, was defended by a stout wooden door, which is still in place, and an iron " yett ", of which only the hinges remain. The ground floor of the entrance tower is almost entirely occupied by the stair to the first floor, the narrow room behind it having been the guardroom, or possibly a prison.

The main stair ended at the first floor, and two spiral stairs in the angles on the north side between the towers and the main block led to the upper floors. These stairs account for the distinctive appearance of Glenbuchat's exterior, for instead of being carried on corbels, as was customary in Scotland at that time, the turrets are supported by arches, a characteristic more often found in France. A possible explanation may be that when Sir Robert Carnegie, the father of Helen, was ambassador to the Court of Henri II, he came under French architectural influence.

The great hall once covered the entire first floor of the main block, but was later divided into two. An extra storey was also contrived by lowering the ceiling of the hall, a work which necessitated the insertion of extra windows.

The last Gordon laird of Glenbuchat was a colourful character, who in his youth was a student with another lively rogue, Simon Fraser, Lord Lovat. " Old Glenbucket " is said to have given George II nightmares, and undoubtedly played an active part in both the Jacobite risings. In 1715 he had some success against the Hanoverian troops and fumed at the inefficiency of other supporters of the Old Pretender. He was imprisoned for a time at Edinburgh, but continued to dabble in intrigue until he joined Prince Charles Edward in '45 and become one of his principal advisers. After the collapse of the '45, he took to the hills with a sizeable price on his head, but managed, although seventy years of age, to escape to Norway by boat, and then to Sweden by sled. He lived the last years of his life in exile in France, at the court of the Stuarts he had done his best to serve.

KILDRUMMY

Kildrummy, although much of the fabric is so ruinous that only the foundations remain, is among the most interesting of Scottish castles. It is possible to follow the ground-plan in some detail, from which it is clear that Kildrummy was in its final stages an elaborately constructed fortification.

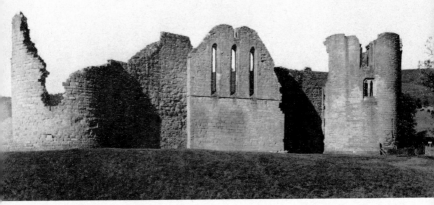

Kildrummy Castle

The site is a strong one, protected by a ravine to the north. The curtain is pentagonal, with the gatehouse at the most salient angle and a round tower at each of the other four corners. Of these, the western tower was the keep, while the eastern, or Warden's Tower is the most complete. The earliest building is generally attributed to Gilbert de Moravia, Bishop of Caithness from 1223–45, during the reign of Alexander II, and it may be to this ecclesiastical origin that Kildrummy owes its greatest peculiarity.

The chapel, so that it shall be properly orientated liturgically, breaches the eastern curtain wall, and, although constructed at first-floor level, this together with the three lancet windows must have proved a serious weakening of the defences. It is significant that the foundations of a further round tower, obviously never completed, have been discovered beyond the curtain at this point.

The gatehouse, of which again nothing but the foundations remain, was clearly Edwardian in style, with two great flanking drum towers. It is generally assumed to have been built about 1290, and may have

been the work of Master James of St. George, the architect of Conway, Caernarvon and Harlech. Certainly, Edward I stayed at Kildrummy in 1296, at which time he may have ordered the erection of the tower outside the chapel.

Kildrummy has had a troubled history. The then owner, the Earl of Mar was married to a sister of Robert Bruce, so it was only to be expected that Kildrummy should be held for the Bruce during his campaign against the English. In 1305, Edward I decreed that the castle should be governed by a reliable officer, a command which seems to have had little effect, as it was to Kildrummy that the defeated Bruce sent his Queen for safety. In the late summer of 1306, the castle suffered a two months' siege conducted by Prince Edward of Caernarvon (Edward II), which ended, through the treachery of a blacksmith, in the surrender of the garrison and the execution of the Commander, Sir Nigel Bruce, Robert's brother.

Osborne, the blacksmith, had fired the castle, but it was repaired, and in patriot hands again by 1335, when Bruce's sister, Dame Christian, defended it against the supporters of Baliol. It was relieved by Dame Christian's husband, Sir Andrew Moray, who demolished the keep, in accordance with Bruce's policy of leaving no stronghold which might benefit the English.

Kildrummy suffered another siege when David II was in conflict with the Earl of Mar, and for a time it became Crown property. James III presented it to his luckless favourite, Robert Cochrane, who was captured and hanged by Earl Archibald " Bell-the-Cat " Douglas. During the Civil Wars it was garrisoned first for the King and then for Parliament. It was fired yet again at the accession of William III, and was dismantled for the last time after the 1715 rebellion, during which it served as headquarters for the Earl of Mar.

Angus

CLAYPOTTS

There are other examples of oddly constructed castles in Scotland and elsewhere, but one of the most curious is the Z-plan tower of Claypotts. The ground plan conforms to the general rule, with a rectangular central block and two round towers at diagonally opposed corners; the peculiarity lies in the heavy corbelled overhang at the summit of the flanking towers, an effect achieved by placing a square top storey on a round base. There would seem to be no functional reason for this apart from decoration.

Claypotts Castle

The tower was built for the Strachans of Claypotts, probably between 1569 and 1588, the dates on the south and north towers, and despite its late period was obviously intended for defence. The flanking towers are liberally supplied with gunports—one being placed in the kitchen fireplace—and the only window in the lower storeys is to be found in the kitchen.

In Z-plan towers it was not uncommon for one flanking tower to be devoted entirely to the staircase, but at Claypotts two spiral stairs have been built at the junction of the round towers with the main block. The round towers, five storeys high to the four of the central one, are devoted entirely to additional storage and living space. Another slightly odd feature of Claypotts is that the rooms in the round towers are square on every floor, and not, as might have been expected, only in the overhang.

The castle was occupied for a time by Graham of Claverhouse, known as " Bonnie Dundee " to his admirers and " Bloody Clavers " to the less enthusiastic. He was killed at the Battle of Killiecrankie in 1689.

GLAMIS

The history of Glamis stretches back into antiquity, long before the building of even the oldest part of the present castle. The story of

15

William Shakespeare's play, *Macbeth* is probably known to almost every school child, as is the legend of the haunted chamber and its mysterious occupant. In the twentieth century, Glamis Castle is famous as the birthplace of Queen Elizabeth the Queen Mother and Princess Margaret.

It is probable that the site of the castle was fortified when it was presented in 1376 to John Lyon, Lord Glamis, on the occasion of his marriage to the daughter of Robert II. It was John Lyon who began the building which forms the nucleus of the castle of today. Strange as it may seem, hidden beneath the towers and ornamentation of later centuries, is an L-plan tower. The keep was originally four storeys high with an embattled parapet, of which some of the corbels are still in existence. The 10 feet thick walls of the keep contained a number of small rooms, the well and, of course, the garderobes. The interior of the keep has been considerably altered, but it is possible to trace the original layout, and the entrance is still defended by an iron yett.

Later extensions transformed Glamis to an approximation of a Z-plan tower. Patrick, Earl Glamis (1578–1615), erected a large wing at the south-east angle of the keep with a round tower at the corner; the work seems to have been completed by his son, John, whose monogram appears over one of the west windows.

The matching north-west wing was built in the seventeenth century and reconstructed in the nineteenth. Surmounting the keep is an erection of frankly top heavy appearance. It is two storeys high and is highly ornate with a multitude of angle turrets. The whole is typical of seventeenth century Scottish castellation, a style which, though tolerable in its genuine state, deteriorated only too easily into the unattractive Scottish Baronial of the nineteenth century.

Argyllshire

DUNSTAFFNAGE

Dunstaffnage stands on a promontory jutting into Loch Etive. The curtain is roughly quadrangular, following the line of the site so exactly that there is no possible foothold on the rocks outside the walls. The castle dates from the mid-thirteenth century and is in relatively good condition, the walls rising to some 60 feet above ground level, or thirty above the courtyard.

The entrance, at the eastern angle of the quadrangle, is about 20 feet above ground level and was approached by a flight of steps with a drawbridge at the summit. The entrance has been much reduced in

Glamis Castle

size at various times and a tower-house was built above it in the seventeenth century.

The keep, round to the field and square to the enceinte, stands at the western angle of the castle on the highest part of the rock. It was three storeys high, with its ground floor six feet above the level of the courtyard. A similarly shaped tower at the northern angle seems to have been approached only from the battlements. Unfortunately, it is almost impossible to deduce what the internal arrangement of the two towers was, but a range of domestic buildings, including a kitchen, of indisputably early date lies between them.

Two hundred yards away from the castle are the ruins of a chapel which shows every sign of having been built at the same time. Thus, the lancet windows are identical in style with those in the curtain, and there is reason to suppose that the men who built the chapel also built the castle.

Dunstaffnage Castle

Sween Castle

SWEEN

Sween is one of, if not the oldest stone castle in the Kingdom of Scotland, and, as might be expected is of primitive design. It stands, a simple quadrangular enclosure dating from the twelfth century, upon the east shore of Loch Sween. The wall is featureless, save for a buttress at each corner and in the middle of each side, though a square tower was added to the north-east angle in the thirteenth century, and a round one to the north-west in the sixteenth. The entrance which is by a round arch in the centre of the south wall was originally secured by a door fastened by a draw-bar.

The interior of the enclosure is empty except for a well, but round the inside of the wall runs a groove which could have had no other purpose than to support a timber floor. Thus, the walls of Sween are, contrary to all appearances, not curtains surrounding a bailey, but the walls of the keep itself.

Bute

ROTHESAY

The shell keep, a common enough feature of English military architecture is virtually unknown in Scotland, hence the particular interest of Rothesay. The oldest part of the castle is the circular curtain wall, which may well date from the middle of the twelfth century. At this time the entrance was by a simple breach in the curtain, but in the thirteenth century a forework to accommodate a portcullis and a gate was added. At the same time the castle was further strengthened by the four equidistant round towers built outside the curtain.

James IV and James V built a new and massive forework, thrusting far beyond the thirteenth-century addition, which comprised a barbican, gateway and great hall. A small postern was inserted to the west of the curtain, and the walls were heightened several feet. When this was done, the old parapet was not destroyed, and the line of the original battlements is clearly visible, sealed up within the later masonry.

The only building still standing within the enceinte has a chapel on the upper floor.

Rothesay was besieged by the Norsemen in 1230. The Scots poured boiling pitch and lead upon the attackers, but the Norse pressed forward, covering themselves with wooden shields, and we are told contrived to hack their way with axes through the soft stone of the walls. The castle was destroyed by Argyll in 1685.

Rothesay Castle

Rothesay Castle from the air   [Aerofilms Ltd.

Dumfriesshire

CAERLAVEROCK

Caerlaverock is something of a mystery castle since architecturally it has much in common with the Welsh Edwardian castle, while its early history indicates that it must be of Scottish construction. It can hardly have been built before 1280, and in 1299 the head of its Scottish constable was impaled upon the walls of nearby Lochmaben tower by the English commander. Edward I conducted a brisk and classic siege in 1300, in the course of which his catapults hurled stones both night and day. The garrison put up a spirited resistance, but finally capitulated when reduced to sixty men. The castle was recaptured and dismantled, by Bruce. Its owner, Sir Eustace Maxwell, received compensation from the Crown. It was subsequently rebuilt and then dismantled again in 1356. It was rebuilt again in about 1400 and added to in the seventeenth century.

Edward's siege was commemorated in a poem by Walter of Exeter, who was present at the time. According to this poem, the castle, shaped like a shield, i.e. triangular, with a tower at each corner, has undergone little basic alteration during the successive rebuildings. It stands on a rock on the north shore of the Solway, at the mouth of the Nith. Surrounded by a wide moat, which, in its turn, is bounded by an earthen rampart, the defences are concentric. The whole is set in the midst of a marsh, the only approach being by the firm land to the north, at which point stands the forward-thrusting gatehouse.

With its two great flanking towers, the gatehouse is the earliest example of the keep-gatehouse in Scotland, although it has undergone considerable alterations, both internally and externally. The machicolations for instance are of fifteenth century construction. The walls of the portcullis room between the towers are grooved for the hoisting machinery of portcullis and drawbridge. Originally the main domestic buildings were also contained in the gatehouse, but in later centuries considerable extensions were made along the walls of the courtyard.

In the early sixteenth century a two-storey building was ranged against the west wall, the curtain was heightened by several feet and a window, the only opening in this wall, was inserted. The finest of the later buildings is the block along the east wall erected by Robert, Lord Maxwell, created first Earl of Nithsdale in 1620. The magnificent façade, its windows richly ornamented with heraldic carvings and sculptures illustrating tales from the classics, is typical of early Renaissance work in Scotland. The curtain is pierced by windows on this side, indicating that security was no longer of maximum importance.

Caerlaverock Castle

Nevertheless, the castle was besieged by the Covenanters in 1640, though it remained the seat of the Earls of Nithsdale until 1716. The then Earl took part in the Jacobite Rebellion of 1715, was captured and sentenced to death but, through the courage of his wife, contrived to escape from the Tower of London. He ended his days in exile and the castle became a ruin.

A fortification some 300 yards to the south of the present building has been the subject of much controversy, but is now believed to be the remains of a primitive earthwork.

East Lothian

CRICHTON

Crichton is a good example of the way in which the courtyard castle grew up around the early tower-house.

Crichton Castle

There is no record of the building of the keep, a rectangular tower probably dating from the late fourteenth century, and following the traditional plan of stores and dungeon at ground-floor level and great hall above. There is an outside entrance to the ground floor and a stair to the hall, but no communication direct from the hall to the chambers beneath. An unusual feature is the positioning of the tiny kitchen partly hollowed out of the thickness of the wall in an entresol, above the dungeon and just below the hall. The dungeon exhibits only too clearly one of the more unpleasant sides of mediaeval life: it measures about eight feet by six, is ventilated by a narrow slit in the outer wall, and has its door, which is only thirty inches high, some eight feet above the floor.

Sir William Crichton, Chancellor to James I and guardian of the young James II, was probably responsible for the first extensive rebuilding after the partial destruction of the castle in 1445. To this period belong the new great hall in the south wing and the large kitchens in the west wing. A stalwart tower was erected at the south-west angle, its walls so thick that it was long thought to be the original keep: as, however, it is the only part of the castle with no vaulted floors, having been divided throughout by timber floors, its more likely purpose was the provision of private chambers, such as bedrooms.

In 1488, Crichton was granted to Patrick Hepburn, first Earl of Bothwell, and it later became a favourite residence of James Hepburn, Mary Stuart's Bothwell. Here his sister married John Stewart, the

Queen's half-brother, and a wedding-feast was held, at which 1800 deer were cooked. Not, one imagines, in the kitchen of the keep!

To Crichton, Bothwell took his own bride, Jean Gordon, and it became part of her portion after the divorce which enabled her husband to marry the Queen.

To Francis Stewart, fifth Earl of Bothwell, Crichton is indebted for its most distinctive feature. The Earl had spent some time in Italy, and the seven bay arcade along the north wing was clearly inspired by his residence there. Although quite unique and, with the square facets on the wall above, not unattractive, it cannot be denied that Francis Stewart's innovation looks out of place beneath sunless northern skies. The pillars are decorated with a monogram made up of the Earl's initials, those of his wife, Margaret Douglas, and an anchor, indicating that Francis Stewart, like James Hepburn, was Lord High Admiral of Scotland.

James VI was entertained at Crichton in the days before the Earl fell from favour for plotting against the Crown and, furthermore, practicing witchcraft in pursuit of his treasonable ends.

DIRLETON

There is an allusion to the castle of Dirleton as early as 1225, but the fabric of the oldest part of the existing building is probably the work of John de Vaux, seneschal to Marie de Coucy, who married Alexander II

Dirleton Castle

in 1239. The Lord of Coucy had a formidable castle, and a high officer to his daughter would almost certainly have had a stronghold of note.

The cluster of towers to the south of the site is unique in Scottish military architecture. Although the entire concentration of towers (two round and one square) should be considered as a single unit, the largest round tower formed the donjon. Originally there was another square tower on the courtyard side of the group, so that the whole was virtually a castle within a castle.

The apartments in the donjon are polygonal. The lord's hall retains its rather primitive stone vault and has a hooded fireplace enriched with dog-tooth moulding.

The curtain, which had two further flanking towers, closely followed the line of the site, a natural mound of no great height, surrounded by a wide moat. The castle was held for Wallace in 1298, when it was besieged for Edward I by that redoubtable prelate, Anthony Bek, Prince-Bishop of Durham. After its capture it suffered much damage, but the remaining fabric was incorporated in the rebuilding.

The fourteenth-century gateway is well preserved, and exhibits practically every form of mediaeval fortification. The moat was spanned by a bridge which terminated some 11 feet short of the castle, the rest of the gap being negotiated by a drawbridge. The entrance was defended by gates, a portcullis, machicolation, and a meurtrière in the floor of the portcullis room.

The main addition of the fifteenth century was the range along the eastern curtain. The ground floor, which is hewn out of solid rock, contains the bakery, cellars and well. Above is a fine kitchen with two fireplaces and a service room leading into the hall. This was 72 feet long by 25 wide and contains an unusual concession to comfort in the shape of a canopied stone seat backing onto the kitchen fireplace. The lord's rooms, at the north end of the range, were built over the guard-room and the dungeon, this last being accessible only through a trap-door.

The castle has been a ruin since 1650, when it was besieged and finally dismantled by General Monk. At the time it was said to be " a nest of moss-troopers " but Dirleton met its end gallantly for, when the garrison surrendered to an army of 1600, it consisted of less than 70 men.

TANTALLON

Red stone on a rocky promontory, against the background of the North Sea, Tantallon is one of the most strikingly beautiful of castles. Such is the invulnerability of the site, for the rocks rise sheer some 100 feet from

Tantallon Castle

the sea, that only a short stretch of curtain across the neck of the promontory was considered necessary. Beyond this, to landward was a triple line of ditches.

The great curtain, 50 feet high and 12 feet thick, dates from about 1350. At either extremity are the remains of a round tower, now only fragmentary but once rising another 20 feet above the parapet. In the centre is the keep-gatehouse, from which the walls slope back slightly. The walls themselves are battlemented but without machicolation.

Originally, the curtain was riddled with small chambers, and passages. However, in 1528, at which time the castle belonged to the Douglases, Tantallon was besieged by James V, who had no love for the then owners. James's bombardment failed, but nevertheless the castle was surrendered to him—gold possibly proving stronger than cannon-balls— and the King ordered considerable alterations.

The walls, which had already proved impregnable, were further strengthened by the filling in of all hollow spaces: this work was done with blocks of green basalt, in dramatic contrast to the red sandstone. The entrance tower was supplied with gun embrasures and the old gateway was blocked, leaving only a small door and narrow passage.

Although the keep, over 40 feet square, must have given ample accommodation, inevitably there were extensions within the enceinte. The principal addition was the wing to the north of the promontory, which included storage rooms, a hall, bedrooms and other private apartments. There are traces of some building on the south side, but if any existed to the east (the side facing the curtain) they have completely vanished.

Tantallon was destroyed by the Covenanters in 1639.

YESTER

Yester castle, which dates from the mid-thirteenth century, stands on a promontory at the junction of Hopes Water and a stream. It was triangular on plan, but little now remains above ground, except for a stretch of the curtain cutting off the tip of the promontory and a section of the eastern wall. The north wall (across the tip) was built without flanking towers and without any opening except for a postern gate. The approach was from the south, where a wide ditch had the effect of turning the promontory into an island. The gatehouse, of which only the foundations remain, seems to have had two flanking towers.

The remarkable feature of Yester is in fact not visible at all from above. Just outside the north curtain is an underground chamber known as Goblin Hall which is reached by a flight of steps down from the enceinte. It is about 37 feet long by 13 wide with a high-pointed vaulted roof and was originally divided into two storeys by a timber floor. At the south end of the hall there are doors at both levels, the upper one of which must have been accessible from a passage off the stair leading from the courtyard. On the upper floor there is a fireplace in the north wall, while on the lower, at the north end of both the side walls there is another door. The west door gives onto a steeply sloping passage, defended by three doors and probably by a portcullis as well, leading to the bank of the stream. The passage from the east door ends against a rock face; there is a stair down leading to the well, but it is unlikely that either stair or passage was ever completed.

The Host in Scott's *Marmion* says that Goblin Hall was built by supernatural means:—

> Of lofty roof and ample size,
> Beneath the castle deep it lies.
> To hew the living rock profound,
> The floor to pave, the arch to round,
> There never toil'd a mortal arm—
> It all was wrought by word and charm.

The truth, unfortunately, is more mundane, since Mr Stewart Cruden, HM Inspector of Ancient Monuments for Scotland, suggests that Goblin Hall was the undercroft of a tower which was removed to make way for a later rebuilding of the castle.

Lochleven Castle

Fife

LOCHLEVEN

Because of its associations with Mary, Queen of Scots, Lochleven is, at least by name, one of the most famous of Scottish castles. It comes, therefore, as a surprise to see its extreme simplicity and relatively small dimensions. The external measurements of the keep are only about 30 feet by 24, while the enceinte could with some justification, by reason of its smallness, be called a barmkin.

The exact date of building is not known, but in 1335 the castle was defended by Alan de Vipont against John de Strivilin, a supporter of Edward Baliol, and both keep and curtain show every sign of dating at least from that time. The single drum tower at the south-east corner of the enceinte was a sixteenth-century addition, and there have been other buildings within the courtyard.

The keep, now gutted, was five storeys high, with three bartizans but no machicolation. Entrance was by means of a ladder to the second floor, where the door was secured by draw-bars. The only access to the first floor was by an interior stair from the entrance floor, while the basement was reached by a trapdoor in the floor above.

Lochleven Castle
(*a closer view*)

One of the windows has been fitted with a stone slab, traditionally said to have served as an altar during the imprisonment of Mary Stuart. The Queen was held at Lochleven for nearly a year, during 1567–68, when she was in the custody of Lady Margaret Douglas, the mother of her half-brother, the Earl of Moray. It was there that she signed her abdication and gave birth to still-born twins, the children of Bothwell. Her undoubted charm won her the support of the younger men of the Douglas family, who effected her escape—one by getting himself banished from the castle on the grounds that his attentions were unpleasant to her, and thus putting himself in a position to get horses and supplies for the flight, the other by stealing the castle keys, which were cast into the the moat by the Queen herself as her young rescuer rowed her across.

RAVENSCRAIG

The promontory castle of Ravenscraig is particularly worthy of note in that it is the first British castle known to have been constructed for defence by artillery. It was started in about 1460 at the command of that pioneer of gunnery, James II, as part of his scheme for coastal defence. Work was held up by the death of the King at Roxburgh, but the castle was completed by his Queen, Mary of Guelders, who devoted a large proportion of her income to it and lived there for much of her widowhood.

On plan it has something in common with Tantallon. The stretch of wall runs across the neck of a promontory jutting into the Firth of Forth, the drop over the rocks forming a natural defence on three sides. In front of the wall, to landward, is a ditch, and the wall terminates at either end in a tower built round to the field and square to the enceinte. The entrance is through a passage in the centre of the curtain, with a guardroom on the left.

The western tower which was the keep and contained the royal apartments can be approached only from the enciente. The eastern tower, which was probably intended primarily for the garrison, connects with the central block, and is built from a lower level than the keep. The rounded sides of both towers are unusually massive, being reinforced to withstand gunfire, and are pierced with gun-ports for the use of the garrison. The ground floors, instead of being used only for storage, were designed as gun emplacements, and across the cellars and entrance passage of the central block runs an open artillery platform, protected to landward by a parapet.

Ravenscraig Castle

St. Andrews Castle

ST. ANDREWS

The Castle of St. Andrews, close to the ruins of the cathedral, was once the episcopal palace, being built in about 1200 by Bishop Roger. Like Tantallon and Ravenscraig, with which on plan it has much in common, it is a promontory fort, though the natural defences are nothing like as formidable as those of the other two castles. It had, however, one great advantage, in that it was possible to revictual it from the sea.

It is pentagonal in shape, with the main defences to the south, or landward side, where the curtain slopes back from the fourteenth century gatehouse. At the north-west and north-east angles stand the remains of two rectangular towers, the Sea Tower and the Kitchen Tower: at each of the southern angles stood a squat round tower, or blockhouse, part of the artillery fortifications of the sixteenth century. A fragment of the south-west blockhouse may still be seen, but the south-eastern has vanished completely; indeed, little remains of the entire eastern range, where erosion has removed both cliff and castle.

In the old gatehouse, the Fore Tower, are embedded parts of Bishop Roger's castle, the cross-wall being that section of the outer wall which included the gateway; this, much reduced in size, forms the present opening in the cross-wall. In 1336 the castle was rebuilt by the English, who were almost certainly responsible for bringing the gatehouse forward, so that it thrust beyond the curtain. This entrance, too, was walled up during the episcopate of Walter Traill (1385–1401), but the portcullis grooves and one of the two slots for the beams of the drawbridge are clear evidence of its position.

Bishop Traill rebuilt much of the curtain, and inserted a new entrance in the range to the west of the Fore Tower. Bishop Traill's curtain is now the inner wall of this south-west range, the outer wall dating from the sixteenth century, and his gateway is the arch at the inner end of what is now the entrance passage.

The Fore Tower in its final form was a handsome rectangular building, four storeys high, with an ornately corbelled parapet. The range to the west of the tower comprised the entrance passage, with a vaulted chamber on either side, and, it would seem, a long hall on the first and second floors. The ground floor of the eastern range opened onto a loggia which faced north. Crichton has a similar amenity, but one wonders how often the owners of either castle were able to profit from their Italianate status symbols. On the floor above was the chapel, though this is more easily to be deduced from the study of an eighteenth print than from the present state of the ruins.

The northwest Sea Tower contains a particularly unpleasant prison, the Bottle Dungeon, so called from its shape. It is hollowed out of the rock to a depth of 24 feet, and is reached by a hole in the floor of the cell above. George Wishart, the Protestant leader, was imprisoned in the dungeon before being burnt outside the castle in 1546, while other political prisoners vanished into its depths, never to reappear.

St. Andrews is, unfortunately, in a more ruinous state than many other castles of equal importance. It has suffered much through the fortunes of war, but even more from erosion and the removal of stones which were used to repair the harbour.

St. Andrews suffered two major sieges. In 1337 it was attacked by Sir Andrew Moray on behalf of David II: Sir Andrew was the brother-in-law of the late king, Robert Bruce, and took care to render the castle untenable, so that it was a ruin until Bishop Traill repaired it.

From 1539–46, Cardinal David Beaton was Archbishop of St. Andrews. A fanatical Catholic and a man of considerable political ambitions, he incurred the hatred of the rising Protestant party—it was he who was largely responsible for the execution of Wishart. A small force of Protestants, including John Knox, gained possession of the castle and murdered the Cardinal, hanging his body by two sheets from the window of one of the towers (traditionally the Fore Tower, but Knox, who should have known, tells us it was the south-east blockhouse). Henry VIII, engaged in war with Scotland, supported the Protestants, who managed to hold out for a year, until the French fleet intervened on behalf of the Regent, Marie of Guise. The castle was once more badly damaged and Knox spent two years in the galleys.

33

An interesting reminder of this siege demonstrates also a technique of contemporary warfare. The Regent's forces, under the Earl of Arran, attempted to mine the castle, tunnelling from a point south-east of the Fore Tower, and establishing a minehead from which they intended to continue with several subsidiary passages until the foundations were breached. The scheme was not carried through, as the defenders sank a counter-mine, which with remarkable luck or accuracy came out in the attackers' minehead. Before this successful attempt, however, they had sunk trial shafts in the chambers on either side of the entrance passage.

The unfortunate Beaton was succeeded as Archbishop by John Hamilton, who was to have little more luck. He was executed in 1571 for his part in the civil wars of the first years of the reign of James VI, but not before he had repaired the devastation of the siege of 1546–47. His badge, a five-pointed star appears above the entrance arch and on a panel on the Fore Tower. He was the last to make any major alterations to the castle and, from the mid-seventeenth century onwards, it was allowed to fall into disrepair.

Kisimul Castle

Inverness

KISIMUL, BARRA

The earliest record of this land fortress dates from the first part of the fifteenth century, but it was almost certainly built prior to this. The castle consists of a solid four-storey keep and an irregularly shaped curtain, rising sheer from the rock. There are no slits or windows in the curtain and very few in the walls of the keep, so that defence must have been conducted entirely from the parapet. The curtain is pierced by holes for the beams of an hoarding, an indication that the castle is pre-fifteenth century, built before the timber hoarding had been superseded by stone machicolation. The parapet walk was probably also made of timber, there being no evidence of a stone walk ever having existed.

There was no gatehouse. It may be supposed that the sea formed an adequate defence, so the entrance was through a simple passage breaching the curtain at the angle of the keep. Two small semi-circular flanking towers complete the defences. As was customary, buildings (now ruined) were built at a much later date within the courtyard.

Kincardineshire

DUNNOTTAR

The building of the tower at Dunnottar is said to have resulted in the excommunication of Sir William Keith for profaning church lands, since the site had been occupied by a church. The dispute was settled after an appeal to the Pope, but Sir William had to build a new church.

He can hardly be blamed for having elected to build his tower where he did, for the site must have been almost impregnable. It is washed on three sides by the sea and only a short stretch of curtain wall was necessary. The approach was made by means of a steep cliff path to the point at which the gateway made the only break in the wall.

The oldest part of the castle is Sir William's L-shaped keep, dating from about 1395, though the corbelled parapet may well be later. The main block contains the usual basement prison and store, the common hall on the first floor and the lord's hall and private apartments above. The original kitchen was on the first floor of the wing, and was fitted with a large fireplace and oven and a sink and drain. Later the kitchen was transferred to the former basement store, where a fireplace was inserted.

A variety of buildings, including a chapel, a bakehouse and a brewhouse grew up within the enceinte, but the most impressive range is that known as " Waterton's Lodgings ". This was erected by George Keith, fifth Earl Marischal (the founder of Marischal College, Aberdeen), in the late sixteenth century, when more ample accommodation was required for the housing of guests and members of the household. It consists of seven ground-floor chambers, each with its own doorway, fireplace and window overlooking the courtyard, and a long gallery above. The last addition to the buildings was the wing at the north-east corner of the quadrangle, which was intended for stores but is better remembered for having been used as a prison for Covenanters.

There are gun batteries facing out to sea on the east and north sides and gun-loops form part of the fortification of the entrance. Most of the artillery was removed after the castle surrendered to General Lambert in 1652. The besiegers had hoped to capture the crown jewels, the Honours of Scotland, which had been deposited in the castle, but the defenders had contrived to smuggle them out to a place of concealment in the parish church of Kinneff.

The Earls Marischal were supporters of the Stuart cause. Earl William Keith who became Lord Privy Seal after the Restoration entertained Charles II at Dunnottar. A later Earl joined the Old Pretender in 1715, after which the castle was dismantled.

Kirkcudbrightshire

THREAVE

Threave is a typical example of a late fourteenth-century tower-house. It stands on an island in the River Dee, with the river forming the defences to the west of the castle, while a curtain wall was added on the other three sides at a later date, possibly at the time of Flodden.

The tower, built about 1380 by Archibald the Grim, third Earl of Douglas, is a five storey, rectangular building. The ground floor contains the well, a dungeon and a sink; the kitchen was on the first floor and the great hall on the second. The fourth floor seems to have been used for purposes of defence: the north, south and west walls are pierced for a hoarding and a narrow tunnel runs through the thickness of the wall on all four sides. It has been suggested that this tunnel was just wide enough to allow a man to crawl along it, securing the ends of the beams supporting the hoarding. An alternative theory, put forward by Mr Sidney Toy, is that the tunnel encased the bonding timbers, which have since rotted away, and that the holes, far from being intended for a hoarding, were to accommodate pigeons.

Much of the curtain has vanished, but it was strengthened by three drum towers at the angles.

Threave Castle

The Douglases were a powerful family, often at odds with the Crown, and the castle suffered a notable siege in 1455, when James II attacked it with Mons Meg, the famous gun of Edinburgh Castle. Threave was finally destroyed in 1640.

Lanarkshire

BOTHWELL

In a country famed for its castellation, there are few finer examples than Bothwell, perched on a steep bank above the River Clyde, and in its day one of the most important castles in the country. As such, it changed hands continuously during the late thirteenth and early fourteenth centuries. It seems to date from about 1270–80 and to have been built by the de Moravia family (the Morays), but by 1298 it was in the hands of the English, since it then suffered a fourteen-month siege by the Scots, who eventually regained it.

However, in 1301 it was captured by Edward I after a brief but spectacular siege. Edward had constructed at Glasgow a vast siege-engine known as a belfry. This was a wooden tower on wheels with a

Bothwell Castle

drawbridge at the summit, which could be pushed against the walls of a defending castle and thus permit the attackers to gain the ramparts with comparative ease. Edward's belfry for the siege of Bothwell needed thirty carts to transport it and the eight-mile journey from Glasgow took two days, along a specially constructed road.

Bothwell remained in English hands until after the battle of Bannockburn, when it was surrendered to Edward Bruce and dismantled in accordance with the " scorched earth " policy of Robert Bruce. By 1336 it was again occupied by the English, who were finally ejected in March 1337, by the true owner, Sir Andrew Moray, Warden of Scotland. Nevertheless, he was forced to " scatter it from the foundations " according to a contemporary chronicler, though it is likely that this meant no more than the demolition of half the donjon tower. The castle seems to have been left a ruin until about 1371, when Archibald the Grim, third Earl of Douglas acquired it and transformed it into one of his principal strongholds. In 1455, the Douglases forfeited the castle to the Crown: succeeding owners were involved to some degree or other in treasonable activities, and the castle changed hands rapidly, until about 1488, when it was bestowed upon Patrick Hepburn, Lord Hailes (later first Earl of Bothwell), who subsequently exchanged it, at the King's request, for Hermitage Castle.

In 1669, Archibald Douglas, first Earl of Forfar, acquired the castle and pulled down part of it to make room for a new mansion (itself pulled down in 1926), which was completed by the second Earl. He, the last of his line, died in the 1715 rebellion, and the castle became the subject of much legislation. Now, although administered by the Ministry of Works, it is actually the property of the Earls of Home.

With such a chequered history, it is not surprising that much of the castle is difficult to date. It is generally supposed to bear a strong resemblance to the French castle of Coucy, built 1225–42, a most spectacular mediaeval residence, the daughter of whose owner became the queen of Alexander II of Scotland. The dominant feature of Bothwell is the great donjon tower, originally about 65 feet in diameter, nearly 90 feet high and with walls 15 feet thick. As already stated, half the donjon was destroyed, probably by Sir Andrew Moray; in the later rebuilding, no attempt was made to restore the complete circle, but the ruin was simply patched up with a straight wall.

Even in this state, the donjon is a notable piece of military-residential architecture. It is separated from the courtyard by its own moat (this is a feature of Coucy), which was crossed by means of a drawbridge, now destroyed. Although the main entrance is at ground level, security measures were not neglected. An angular projection shelters the doorway and the zig-zag passage leading to the main hall was provided with a portcullis.

The hall was octagonal and probably had a central pier, such as may be seen in the basement. Two fine windows, one in the hall and one at a higher level, overlook the courtyard. The basement, which contains a well, can only be reached from above. The garderobes for the donjon are contained in the thickness of the south curtain wall: the flue descends so as to be flushed by the waters of the moat, and a passage at the base leads into the moat. The breach in the wall is divided by a central pillar, obviously intended to deter any attempt to enter the donjon at this point.

At intervals along the curtain wall stand the small round south-west tower which contained the prison, a small square tower, and the large round south-east tower. This last has a handsome machicolated parapet, which is probably contemporary with the adjoining chapel and hall and, therefore, the work of Archibald the Grim or his son. The three-bay chapel, which still has its holy-water stoup and piscina, is connected to the hall by a passage. Both chapel and hall stand at first floor level, and the east curtain was raised when the hall was built.

The square north-east tower is in a very ruinous state, but a print of 1693 shows it as having a machicolated parapet and angle turrets. The inner door had a drawbridge and the masonry is carefully channelled to accommodate the machinery by which it was lifted.

The main gatehouse was probably in the north curtain, but seems to have been destroyed during Lord Forfar's reconstruction. An extension to the north was started but never completed: judging by the remains, it would have included a round tower to the south-east and an imposing if orthodox gatehouse, flanked by round towers, to the north.

Midlothian

BORTHWICK

Borthwick belongs to the later form of tower-house, with extra accommodation provided in wings extending from the central rectangular block: it is unusual, however, in that both wings project from the same side, the west, of the main tower. The castle stands on a tongue of land, jutting into a valley at the junction of two streams, on a roughly rectangular site. The tower is surrounded by a curtain wall, with a massive drum tower defending the gateway and a smaller tower along the south wall. The curtain and the two towers are equipped with gun ports, but these are probably of a later date than the original fabric, and none appear in the tower-house.

The licence to crenellate was granted by James I to Sir William Borthwick in 1430, when he acquired the property of Lochorquhart, which had been the site of a motte-and-bailey castle.

The tower-house, apart from its unusual shape, contains much of interest. The ground floors are largely given over to store-rooms, with a well in the south wing. The north wing contains the small dungeon prison. On the first floor are the main entrance, via a guardroom, the great hall and, in the north and south wings respectively, the kitchen and private apartments. The kitchen has a huge fireplace, with three windows opening into it, a stone sink and a drain. The hall has a fine hooded fireplace and an ornamented bench built into the wall. A unique feature is the canopied washbasin, complete with drain, in the service passage between the kitchen and the hall: a common enough enough feature in English castles, this is exceedingly rare in Scotland.

A carefully constructed garderobe leads from the private apartments in the south wing. If constructed as was usual at this period, to discharge onto the ground, the outlet would have been in unpleasant proximity to the well, so the flue was fitted with movable containers, which could be emptied when necessary.

Immediately above the hall are the drawing-room and the chapel,

Borthwick Castle

the latter being simply a window recess fitted with a piscina and locker. It is, however, noteworthy, in that few except the Scottish royal castles have any chapel at all. The rest of the building contains apartments of various degrees of comfort, intended either for the lord and his family or guests, or for his retainers.

The tower was heavily and ornately machicolated on all sides, but it suffered a siege in 1650, the besieging forces being, it is popularly believed, commanded by Oliver Cromwell in person. The east side of the tower received a severe pounding from the Protector's artillery and the parapet was destroyed. In the subsequent rebuilding, the wall was carried up flush and the machicolation, by this time out-moded, except for decorative purpose, was never replaced.

CRAIGMILLAR

The property of Craigmillar near Edinburgh came into the hands of Simon Preston in 1374, and basically the tower dates from that time. It is a good, if simple, example of the L-plan tower, being a large oblong block with a small projecting wing which housed the guardroom, the kitchen and additional private accommodation.

The original castle seems to have had no curtain wall, but the inner curtain would appear to have been completed by 1427, the date (now

Craigmillar Castle

vanished) once inscribed in the masonry. The castle was sacked by Hertford (later the Protector Somerset) in 1544, during the " rough wooing " of the baby queen, Mary Stuart. Many Edinburgh citizens had deposited their valuables at Craigmillar and the castle was surrendered on condition that no damage was done. Hertford, however, broke his promise, and the outer curtain was probably built subsequently, in order to strengthen the defences. The curtain and its flanking towers are provided with gun-loops which, if they belong to the original fabric and were not inserted later, make Craigmillar the earliest Scottish artillery fortification.

The keep was a formidable affair, built on a rock and with a heavily defended entrance. This is at ground-floor level, in the angle between the main tower and the extra wing: the approach from the gate necessitated going round two sides of the tower and then passing through a narrow passage between the tower and the curtain. Before the door was a cleft in the rock, which was spanned by a drawbridge, and the entrance passage was overlooked by the guardroom. Above the round arch of the doorway are carved the arms of the Prestons.

The interior of the four-storey keep is divided by two stone vaults, which were further divided by two timber floors, the corbels for the support of which still exist. The great hall contains a handsome fireplace, beside which is a carved stone shield, and the large windows at the upper end of the hall have built-in stone seats.

The curtains, about 30 feet high and machicolated, have carved on them the arms of the Prestons and others, as well as the initials of Simon Preston and a rebus (a punning representation) of the family name. Additional buildings were added in the sixteenth century, probably after Hertford's attack, but the carving in the ruined remains of the little chapel lying between the inner and the outer curtain walls indicates that this is of fifteenth century workmanship.

EDINBURGH

Both Edinburgh Castle and the Tower of London play similar parts in the respective histories of Scotland and England. Before the Normans conquered the southern kingdom there was a fortress on Castle Rock in Edinburgh, and even today, the grim walls of the castle dominating the city look as though they have grown out of the living rock. Yet, contrary to all appearances, the present castle is of relatively modern date, most of it having been built after the siege of 1573.

The oldest part of the building is the chapel of St. Margaret. This tiny Norman chapel is situated on the highest part of the rock, and may, indeed, be the oldest building in the city. There is a tradition that the chapel was built during the lifetime of St. Margaret herself, the Saxon princess who became the Queen of Malcolm Canmore, and who died in 1093, the same year in which her husband was slain in battle. It is certainly not later than the reign of David I, the third of the sons of Malcolm and Margaret to wear the crown of Scotland. Square externally, the interior of the east end terminates in the typical Norman apse or semi-circle, and the round chancel-arch is enriched on its west face with bands of zig-zag moulding. After the destruction of the castle in 1314, the chapel, a penthouse above it and an incompleted stable were the only buildings left on the rock. On his deathbed Bruce left orders for the repair of the chapel, but in later centuries it fell into disuse, so that, by the Reformation it was used by the gunners as a store. It was restored drastically in the nineteenth century, but still has many of its original characteristics. It is peculiar in that the side walls are not parallel, so that the east end is nine inches wider than the west, a discrepancy clearly visible in so small a building.

From 1296 until 1313 the castle was in English hands, Edward I having captured it after a siege of eight days. Contemporary records say that the buildings were much damaged, and during the next few years a number of Edward's foremost military architects were actively employed at Edinburgh, among them Walter of Hereford, master mason at Caernarvon. However, in 1313 the castle was captured for Bruce by Thomas Randolph, Earl of Moray. The Scots, led by a former member of the castle garrison, scaled the rock and took the English by surprise. It is said that the Scots guide discovered the path while paying secret nocturnal visits to a girl-friend in the valley.

After this, the castle was laid waste so that it should be of no value to the English if they recaptured it. In 1329 Bruce died, to be succeeded by the child David II, and Scotland's hard-won independence was again in the balance. The coinciding reigns of Bruce, the valiant soldier and the weakling Edward II of England had together enabled Scotland to repel the invaders. Now the positions were reversed, for Edward III, a man of the calibre of his grandfather, Edward I, sat upon the throne of England, and it was not long before the English were again asserting their dubious claims to Scotland. By 1335, Edinburgh was in English hands, and the site, which had been let for pasture land, was the scene of intense building activity. Master John of Kilburn, who also did some work at Bothwell, was one of those employed to build a new hall and " divers other houses " and to repair the curtain wall.

In 1341 the Scots regained the castle by a famous ruse. Under the command of William Douglas, a small party of soldiers were disguised as merchants and contrived to drop their wares in such a way as to prevent the closing of the gates: a larger force, lying in ambush, then seized the opportunity to storm and capture the castle. This time, the Scots managed to hold it, and in 1367 work began on David's Tower, so named after David II.

This tower seems to have been the castle keep, containing royal apartments (in which David died) and a prison. The remains of David's Tower, part of the curtain and a smaller tower are buried in the foundations of the Half-Moon Battery. The Wellhouse Tower, to the north of the rock, was also built in the last part of the fourteenth century, and formed part of the city wall.

The oldest part of the Palace block dates from the fifteenth century, but has been greatly altered, especially in the seventeenth century, so that it is now a fair example of Scottish Renaissance architecture. The King's Lodging lies to the east of the Palace Yard, the Great Hall (now a museum) to the south, and the officers' quarters built in the reign of Queen Anne to the west. The quadrangle is completed by the Scottish War Memorial, built on the site of an eighteenth-century barracks, which in its turn superseded the old Church of St. Mary.

The Stuart Kings made Edinburgh the chief city of their kingdom, and most of them spent long periods, often as prisoners, within the castle. James II as a boy was held there by Chancellor Crichton until his mother, Queen Johanna, smuggled him out, concealed among her clothes. It was at Edinburgh, too, that the young Earl of Douglas and his brother were dragged from the presence of the young king to their summary execution. The Castle was subsequently besieged by the Douglas supporters for nearly a year.

James III was held in honourable captivity in David's Tower in 1482, until his release by his brother, Alexander, Duke of Albany, who had himself had a spell of imprisonment in the same place. James IV built the Great Hall, which has suffered from being used as a barracks and as garrison hospital. The timber roof and the carved stone corbels are still worthy of study: the carving on one of the corbels is thought to be a portrait of James's Queen, Margaret Tudor, the sister of Henry VIII, and another bears James's monogram beneath a crown.

James and the flower of his chivalry died on the field of Flodden, and yet again the King of Scotland was a baby. The fortifications of the castle were repaired and in 1517, James V was brought to the " wyndy and richt unpleasant castell and royk of Edinburgh " for safety's sake. After his childhood, James seems to have spent little time there, but his second wife, Marie de Lorraine, as Regent during the minority of her daughter, Mary, frequently resided in the castle. She died there, worn out after eighteen years of perpetual struggle with the enemies of the Crown, and her body lay in state in St. Margaret's Chapel until it was removed to France for burial.

In the following year, 1561, Mary Stuart visited the castle for the first time, riding up from Holyrood. During the brief years of her actual reign in Scotland she was not infrequently to take refuge there, and it was in a tiny room in the King's Lodging that her son was born. Over the door leading from Palace Yard to this part of the Lodging is a plaque bearing the monogram, M and H, for Mary and Henry (Darnley), and the date, 1566, though it is possible that this was not added until the reign of James VI.

Mary abdicated, but the castle and the city were held for her by Kirkcaldy of Grange, who resisted until, in 1573, a strong force of artillery commanded by Sir William Drury was sent by the English to assist the Regent. Drury's bombardment destroyed the east side of the castle, including David's Tower, and Kirkcaldy was hanged.

The castle now acquired its present form. The visitor still passes through the Regent Morton's portcullis gate, built in 1574, though the three doors and the portcullis have been removed, and the royal arms are a restoration. The Half-Moon Battery, also Morton's work, was built over the ruins of the east wall; it is from here that a gun is fired at 1 pm every day. Throughout the reign of James VI the royal apartments underwent alteration, but the castle came less in use as a palace. Apart from a brief visit by Charles II in 1650, no sovereign entered it until in the nineteenth century George IV descended upon an astonished Edinburgh clad in Highland dress.

The castle's military history was far from over. Sir Patrick Ruthven held it for Charles I against Alexander Leslie, a veteran of the Thirty Years' War, but famine and disease forced him to surrender. In September 1640, his depleted garrison marched out with one flag flying, to the beat of one drum. Both Montrose and Argyll were held prisoner there and Cromwell visited it twice; as a guest in 1648 and to besiege it in 1650, when it was surrendered after three months. The Duke of Gordon held it for James VII (II of England) in 1689, but famine again defeated the garrison.

With its long Stuart history, it might be thought that the castle would have been held for the Jacobites in the '15 and '45 rebellions. True, there was a half-hearted attempt to seize it in 1715, followed in '45 by a slightly more efficient blockade on the part of Charles Edward, but the Stuart supporters who eventually entered the castle did so as prisoners.

No account of the castle can be complete without mention of Mons Meg, most celebrated of guns. She stands outside St. Margaret's Chapel, loved by the tourist, though once she was referred to as the " iron murtherer, Muckle Meg." Cast in Flanders in the fifteenth century, James II used her at the siege of Threave and she fired a salute on the occasion of the marriage of Mary Stuart to the Dauphin. It was firing a salute in honour of the Duke of York (later James VII) that she burst and was left to moulder until 1754, when she was moved to the Tower of London. George IV had her returned to Scotland, and she was brought back to the castle with an escort of cavalry and pipers.

Morayshire

CASTLE DUFFUS

Castle Duffus is an interesting example of the old style motte-and-bailey castle. The site is a low natural ridge with an artificial mound at one end. A wide ditch surrounds the bailey wall, enclosing, in all, about nine acres of land, and it has been suggested that this is even older than the castle, having once formed part of a primitive fort.

The curtain appears to have been polygonal without flanking towers, and of no great height. The interesting feature is undoubtedly the keep, which is a classic example of the folly of building a square stone tower on top of a circular artificial mound. The weight of stone proved too much for the motte and one corner of the tower has collapsed and slipped down the motte. It is tribute to the skill of the masons, however, that the broken-away wall is still more or less intact. The internal arrangements of the tower cannot now be determined, except that it consisted of three floors, and that the stair ascended to the left of the entrance. There are traces of a ditch running between the motte and the curtain wall.

The keep is difficult to date, though the shape of the basement windows

Castle Duffus

indicates the early fourteenth century. Certainly in 1305, Sir Reginald de Cheyne, who had acquired the castle through marriage from the de Moravia family, was granted 200 oaks by Edward I " to build his manor of Dufhous ". This would seem an excessive amount of timber for the construction of a stone castle, yet it is hardly conceivable that Sir Reginald would be building at this late period an old style wooden castle. Duffus remains, therefore, an interesting subject for historical research and conjecture.

COXTON

Coxton has been called, with justification, one of the most remarkable buildings in Scotland. Despite its appearance of belonging to an earlier age there is no reason to believe that it is any older than the date carved above the doorway, 1644, the year in which it was completed for Sir Alexander Innes. It is actually more of a fortified manor than castle, though its walls are five feet thick, its outer door guarded by a yett, and its walls pierced by gunloops.

It is a square tower, 53 feet high, divided into four floors, with only one room to each floor. Entrance was by means of a ladder to the first floor, though an outer stair was built at a later date. The ground-floor store could be reached either by an outer door, or by a trapdoor from the first floor. A narrow stair in the thickness of the wall led to the upper chambers.

The tower is surmounted by three angle turrets, two round with conical roofs, the third square, open to the sky and machicolated. South of the Border, this type of architecture would have been considered unbearably old-fashioned, but in many ways Scotland was still living in the Middle Ages, and the seventeenth century was nearly over before the last of these tower-houses was built.

Coxton Tower

Cawdor Castle

Nairnshire

CAWDOR

The history of Cawdor castle goes back considerably further than the existing structure, there being two entries in the fourteenth-century Exchequer Rolls for expenses incurred at " Calder Castle ". The association with the Macbeth story, and the murder of Duncan, belongs to legend, since the real Duncan met his death in battle in 1040.

Most of the present building is comparatively modern, but the central tower dates at least from 1454, when the licence to crenellate was granted to the Calders of Calder by James II. The King reserved the right of entry to the castle for himself and his heirs, while granting the owners the right to build " walls and ditches and [to] equip the summit with turrets and means of defence, with warlike provisions and strengths."

The castle stands on a steep bank on the Cawdor Burn, a tributary of the River Nairn, and was guarded on the landward side by a dry ditch. The rectangular keep occupies the highest part of the site and was surrounded by a curtain wall, some parts of which may have been incorporated in the later extensions. The keep was originally four floors high, with the entrance (now blocked in) at first-floor level. The new door, slightly above ground level, still retains the iron yett, said to have been brought by the Thane of Cawdor from the dismantled castle at Lochindorb. In the basement is the trunk of a thorn tree, which is supposed to have grown on the site before the tower was built around it.

The upper part of the keep was remodelled in the seventeenth century, when the roof was altered. The angle turrets, which are circular below and octagonal above, with conical roofs, may also have been reconstructed, the circular lower part representing the original open bartizan.

From the sixteenth to the nineteenth centuries the castle underwent constant renovations and additions. Particularly noteworthy are the great hall in the north range and the great chamber in the west, both of which contain fine fireplaces. Cawdor also possesses a secret chamber in which the notorious Simon Fraser, Lord Lovat (the last man to be executed on Tower Hill), is said to have hidden after the collapse of the 1745 Jacobite Rebellion.

Orkney

NOLTLAND, WESTRAY

A formidable fortress, on an almost impregnable site is Noltland on the

Noltland Castle

island of Westray. It is a Z-plan structure, with a rectangular central block and square flanking towers, one of which contains the main stair and the other private rooms and garderobes. The most striking feature of Noltland is its superfluity of gun-ports, of which there are at least eighty— this despite the fact that the island has only one safe landing-place, a bay on the east side. The entrance doorway at the angle between the main and the south-west towers, leads onto the main stair, where the visitor is confronted immediately by a gun-port.

Noltland was the property of Gilbert Balfour of Westray, who, since he was involved in the murders of Cardinal Beaton in 1546 and of Darnley in 1567, must have felt the need for a strong fortress. Legend recounts that he was asked to prepare it as a safe refuge for Mary Stuart and Bothwell (who was also Duke of Orkney) after their unpopular marriage. Some of Montrose's officers sheltered at Noltland after the defeat of the Marquis, and the castle was burnt by Cromwell's troops, since when it has remained a ruin.

Doune Castle

Doune Castle: another view

Perthshire

DOUNE

While many, if not most, castles in the British Isles were perpetually being extended and altered, Doune is one of the few that was conceived as a whole. It is a courtyard castle, built for Murdoch, Duke of Albany, Regent for James I during his captivity in England and executed by him in 1424.

The castle lies at the junction of the Teith and the Ardoch on a fairly steep mound, and was further defended by ditches and a now vanished outer wall. The courtyard walls are 40 feet high and topped by a parapet; there is no machicolation, except over a postern in the west wall, but there are open bartizans at the angles and in the centre of the curtain. The main block is ranged against the north wall and has been compared with two tower-houses, set side-by-side.

The entrance to the castle is through a passage running straight through the main block, so that there is no orthodox gatehouse. The passage is flanked on the left by a round tower containing the well, and on the right by the guardroom with its adjoining prison. The portcullis was worked from a recess in the great hall above—an arrangement that must have caused some inconvenience. From the courtyard, access to the great hall was by means of an external staircase. Above the great hall is the great chamber which has a window fitted with a piscina to serve as an oratory.

Another external stair led to the other rooms in the north block, notably the common hall (as opposed to the lord's hall over the entrance) and the kitchen. The entrance lobby has doors into both kitchen and hall and two service hatches from the kitchen. These last have flattened arches of a type much in evidence at Doune but not so common elsewhere.

Above the kitchen and service passage are a number of smaller apartments. There was originally no access from the lord's hall to the common hall though a door was inserted at a later date.

It was obviously intended to build further blocks all round the court-yard. There are large windows in the south wall of the curtain, where it may have been meant to build a chapel. There is some evidence, too, of a projected range against the east wall, but even in its incomplete form, Doune offered ample accommodation by the standards of the time and was never substantially altered.

Hermitage Castle

Roxburghshire

HERMITAGE

Of all the border castles, Hermitage must rank among the finest even though, like Bodiam in Sussex, the almost perfect exterior surrounds nothing but an empty shell. Inevitably, Hermitage changed hands many times and underwent considerable structural alterations, added to which, fact and legend are woven inextricably through its history.

The castle stands amid barren moorland on the north bank of Hermitage Water, surrounded by earthworks which, while basically even older than the oldest parts of the castle, have been altered for artillery. There was some castle on the site in the thirteenth century, the building of which has been attributed both to Nicholas de Soulis and to Walter Comyn, Earl of Menteith—Nicholas has perhaps the better claim, as Hermitage undoubtedly remained for some years in the hands of the de Soulis family. Traditionally, Hermitage came near to causing a war between England and Scotland, when Henry III assembled an army at the border on the grounds that a powerful castle so near the frontier would be a constant threat to the security of his kingdom.

In 1320, Lord William Soulis plotted against the Bruce and forfeited the castle, which passed to an illegitimate son of the King, reverting ultimately to the Crown, though not before it had fallen more than once into the hands of the English. David II granted Hermitage to the Douglas family, who stayed in possession until 1492, when Archibald Douglas, Earl of Angus was suspected of treasonable commerce with the English. With considerable forebearance, James IV demanded only that Angus exchange his border fortress for the less conveniently sited Bothwell castle. Hermitage thus became the property of Patrick Hepburn, Earl of Bothwell and eventually played its part in the tragedy of Mary Stuart. In October 1566, James Hepburn, Earl of Bothwell, Lord of the Marches, who, for all his faults, was always a loyal servant of the Crown, was sorely wounded in an affray with the notorious outlaw, Jock Elliott. Hearing that he was lying at the point of death at Hermitage, Mary Stuart, with one of the rash gestures which were to cost her the Crown and at last brought her to the scaffold, rode in one day from Jedburgh Abbey and back (about 50 miles) to visit him. The fever resulting from this escapade nearly caused Mary's own death, while the scandal set the kingdom in an uproar.

After the disgrace of Francis Stewart, fifth Earl of Bothwell, the castle again reverted to the Crown, passing out of history after its transfer to the Scotts of Buccleuch in the seventeenth century.

It is possible that some small part of the fabric of the existing castle dates from the time of Nicholas de Soulis, but most of the rectangular central block is, somewhat surprisingly, of English origin. In the early fourteenth century, Hermitage was having one of its periods of English ownership, and was in the possession of the Dacre family, who built what was little more than a fortified manor with a small central courtyard.

The warlike Douglases converted and extended until Hermitage became a formidable stronghold. The first addition was a small wing at the south-west angle of the main building, containing the entrance and a portcullis room. Then, in the late fourteenth and early fifteenth centuries, square towers were added to the north-west, north-east and south-east angles; last of all, a larger rectangular tower was built at the south-west angle, absorbing the small entrance wing.

Only the accommodation at ground level in each of the towers can be guessed with any degree of accuracy, though since the south-west tower is so much larger than the others, it probably contained the lord's private apartments. The ground floor, which has a large oven and a curious stone basin, was obviously the kitchen. Both the drain from this and the flues from the garderobes empty into a well-built cesspool with a vaulted roof.

The south-east tower, which has a postern-gate defended by a portcullis, housed the well. In the north-east tower are the prison and a guardroom. Sir Alexander Ramsay, Sheriff of Teviotdale is supposed to have been imprisoned in the dungeon until he starved to death after his capture by Sir William Douglas, in 1342. According to legend, he kept alive for some time by eating the grains of wheat which fell from the granary above, but it is most unlikely that he perished in the present north-east tower.

The basement of the north-west tower contained a cess-pool which drained into the ditch outside, while the first floor seems to have been occupied by garderobes.

From the exterior it is not immediately apparent that Hermitage consists of a group of five towers. The striking features are the tall arches uniting the towers on the east and west sides. Usually, such an arch was built over the entrance, but here the purpose was for defence and there is no gateway at this point. Instead, the arches support a short stretch of wall connecting the upper parts of the towers. The walls are pierced for the beams of a hoarding, and there are doors which would have opened from the top storeys of the towers onto the hoarding. The connecting wall above the arches would thus enable the defenders to throw out their hoarding straight across the east and west faces of the castle, without having to negotiate the narrow recess between the two towers. In the interests of accuracy, it should be added that the eastern arch, which had collapsed, was rebuilt at the beginning of the nineteenth century.

Presumably Hermitage did once have a curtain wall, but if so, every trace of it has vanished, and it may well have been removed when the castle was adapted for use by artillery in about 1540.

Hermitage figures in the grisly tale of the bad Lord Soulis who dabbled in black magic and had a familiar spirit, who told his master that his enemies would never vanquish him

> " Till threefold ropes of sifted sand
> Around thy body twine."

Needless to say, a good magician encompassed the wicked baron's downfall, and he was wrapped in lead and boiled to death. Perhaps because of his activities, Hermitage was believed to have sunk into the ground because of the weight of sin it had gathered about it, and Sir Walter Scott says the peasants of his day regarded its ruins with superstitious dread.

ROXBURGH

Of the ancient city of Roxburgh nothing remains, for after years of perpetual warfare, it was demolished by James II. The fragmentary remains of the great castle, once a rectangle of 400 by 100 yards with massive towers, nothing but a few feet of wall stand on a rock at the junction of the Tweed and the Teviot, near Kelso. There was a fortress at Roxburgh in Saxon times and David I raised it to the status of a royal residence. By 1174, when William the Lion was captured at Alnwick, Roxburgh had become a principal fortress and was forfeited, together with Stirling, Edinburgh and Berwick, as part of the King's ransom.

The castles were restored to the Scots by Richard II, but Roxburgh was handed over to Edward I by Baliol in 1294 and became the prison of Robert Bruce's queen and two sisters. Wallace tried unsuccessfully to regain it, but it was 1314 before Sir James Douglas, a supporter of Bruce, captured it by means of a ruse.

In the twilight, the Scots, their armour concealed under dark robes, approached the castle on all fours and were mistaken by the English for cattle. By 1460, the castle was back in English hands and was besieged by James II, who was killed outside the walls when one of his cannon burst. His queen, Mary of Guelders, rushed to the scene of battle, bringing the young James III with her and inspired the soldiers to press the attack. The castle was stormed and left a ruin until the following century, when temporary repairs were made by Hertford; then, by the terms of the Anglo-Scottish treaty of 1550, Roxburgh castle was finally demolished.

Stirlingshire

STIRLING

Stirling, once one of the four principal Scottish fortresses, has not a little in common with Edinburgh. Both are perched upon high rocks dominating the city, and both, despite their ancient historical background, are in their present form of comparatively recent date. Stirling was an important castle in the twelfth century, when it was one of those pledged to the English in payment of the ransom of William the Lion, after his capture in 1174. By 1304, when it was besieged by Edward I, it was considered among the strongest in the kingdom, and it certainly put up a valiant resistance against the " Hammer of the Scots ".

The garrison, when it surrendered, consisted of only twenty-eight men. Edward had ordered the lead to be stripped from the roofs of the churches of St. Andrews and Dunfermline, so as to make heavier missiles for his siege engines—good churchman as he was, however, he allowed the lead over the altars to be left in position. Even after the surrender, Edward forbade his men to enter the castle until it had been " struck with his war-wolf and that those within the castle defend themselves from the said war-wolf as best they can ". War-wolf appears to have been a new siege weapon, since the Queen and her ladies were among those who watched its demonstration.

The castle then remained in English hands until after Bannockburn, when it was surrendered to Edward Bruce, Robert's brother, and dismantled. During the next reign it changed sides several times, being lost to the Scots after the battle of Halidon Hill (1333), besieged by the Regent, Sir Andrew Moray, in 1337, and recaptured for the last time by the Scots in 1342.

As at Edinburgh, the Stuarts were responsible for much rebuilding. Robert, Earl of Menteith, later Duke of Albany, a son of Robert II, carried out large-scale repairs while Keeper of the Castle. He was succeeded in this office by his son, Murdoch, the builder of Doune castle, who was executed at Stirling in 1424, upon the return of James I from his captivity in England. The King was assassinated in 1437, and one of the men responsible, Sir Robert Graham, was tortured to death at Stirling.

The widowed Queen Johanna took the child King, James II to the castle for safety, but it was not long before Chancellor Sir William Crichton gained possession of his person and carried him off to Edinburgh, from whence the Queen contrived his escape. In later years James committed murder at Stirling. As usual, there was conflict

Stirling Castle

between the Douglases and the Crown, and the King summoned the eighth Earl to meet him at the castle. Although all went well at first, a violent quarrel flared up between the two men, in the course of which James drew his dagger on the Earl. What he had started his courtiers finished, until the lifeless body of the Douglas was flung from the window. The visitor to Stirling can see what is called the Douglas Room, but it was not built until long after this event.

It is generally accepted that James III was born at Stirling, though a rival claim has been put forward by St. Andrews. At all events, James loved Stirling, and from the disastrous years of his reign there grew at least one good thing—the noble Great Hall of his beloved castle. It stands on the eastern side of the inner bailey, once the finest Scottish example of secular Gothic, now, thanks to its eighteenth-century conversion into a barracks, but a ghost of what it must have been. As it was, it consisted of the vast hall itself, with an oak-beamed ceiling, and beneath, the cellars and a brewhouse. The principal entrance was by a covered way from the courtyard of which the Hall forms the east side. At the south end, where the floor was raised slightly, stood the royal dais, with a great fireplace in the wall behind; this end of the Hall was connected by a passage to the King's apartments in the Palace block. The oriel windows retain a few fragments of their former carvings, such as the canopied niches which once contained statues, but for the most part it is only possible to guess at the full glories of James's Hall.

He founded, too, the first Chapel Royal, which, together with the Hall, may have been designed by his architect favourite, Robert Cochrane. This was pulled down to make way for the present Chapel Royal, built by James VI in 1594, for the christening of his elder son, Prince Henry. Its Renaissance façade has suffered little, save for the removal of all royal badges during the Commonwealth. The interior, however, tells the old sad story of conversion to an unsuitable purpose, in this case, an armoury, and though the inserted floors and partitions have now been removed, much has been destroyed which can never be replaced.

The Palace, which forms a great block to the south of the inner bailey, is early Renaissance in style and comparisons have been drawn between it and many of the Loire châteaux. It is built round a central court, known as " the Lion's Den ", where it is possible that James V, during whose reign it was erected, did indeed keep a lion. The Palace obviously had no military value—the great windows alone, despite their iron grilles, would have made it impossible to defend. Between the windows, the wall is recessed slightly, and in each shallow niche stands a tall column, surmounted by a statue. Another row of statues decorates the walls at the level of the parapet. Several are missing or mutilated, but nothing demonstrates more clearly than these statues the difference in outlook between the Middle Ages and the Renaissance. Gone are the stiff, but lovingly portrayed saints and angels of the earlier age. Here stand classical figures, nudes, grotesques, courtiers and warriors: a cross-bowman winds his bow, Venus clasps an arrow and orb, two naked youths brandish sun-blazoned shields. Most interesting is the pseudo-portrait of James V, the bearded figure in doublet and hose, holding a dagger, which is supposed to represent the King in his rôle of the " guid man of Ballengleich ", the disguise in which he went among his subjects.

The Royal apartments, the King's to the north and the Queen's to the south, were on the first floor of the Palace, but like so much else at Stirling, including the entire west side of the inner bailey, have been altered out of recognition.

Mary, Queen of Scots, not yet a year old, was crowned at Stirling, and lived there for several years, until even this refuge was considered not secure enough. Here, too, her son, the future James VI, was christened with great pomp, though such was the breach between his parents at the time, that Mary had to compel her husband to admit the legitimacy of their child. Mary herself narrowly escaped being burned to death in her bed at Stirling, when a candle fired the bed-hangings.

James VI was the last monarch to use Stirling as a royal palace. His own coronation, when he was just over a year old, took place in the parish church of Stirling, and through the war-torn years of his minority, successive Regents strove to hold the custody of both King and castle. James, once he had succeeded to the throne of England, spent little time in Scotland, nor did his son and grandson prove more enthusiastic, though both Charles I and Charles II paid the castle a fleeting visit.

Stirling was attacked by General Monk in the summer of 1651 and received considerable damage, some of which is still visible. During both the 1715 and 1745 rebellions the Jacobite forces made abortive attempts to seize the castle, but were repelled in both instances. With the collapse of the '45, Stirling's active history came to an end, though it is still garrisoned.

For the English student of history, mention may be made of a somewhat incongruous figure among the kings and queens and statesmen who have peopled Stirling. Perkin Warbeck, claiming to be one of the murdered Princes in the Tower and heir to the throne of England, was received there as an honoured guest by James IV, before setting forth on the journey that led him not to the throne, but to the gallows at Tyburn.

West Lothian

NIDDRY

Niddry has little claim to fame, except for its being the place where Mary, Queen of Scots, spent the first night after her escape from Lochleven.

Niddry Castle

The L-plan keep stands on a hillock a few miles from Linlithgow. It was once skirted by a stream, which has been supplanted by the railway-line, while its very mundane present-day background is a slag-heap. The tower was built by George, fourth Lord Seaton, who fell at Flodden in 1513, and it remained in the possession of the Seatons until the reign of Charles I, when it passed to the Hopes of Hopetoun.

The castle is now nothing but a shell, with little to show what the internal arrangements were. At some time in its history it was extended upwards by one floor, the wall of the former parapet being raised to make the wall of the extra storey. The entrance in the re-entering angle, perhaps because it is at ground level, is protected by a forework of slightly later date than the main building.

GLOSSARY

Bailey	Courtyard or ward of a castle
Barbican	Outer defence of a castle or fortified city
Barmkin	Possibly a corruption of barbican. Scottish term for the courtyard of a castle, usually rather smaller than the normal ward or bailey
Bartizan	Overhanging angle turret at the top of a tower
Belfry	Siege engine in the shape of a wooden tower, which could be wheeled against the walls of a besieged fortress, enabling the attackers to reach the summit
Corbel	Stone or timber supporting block, projecting from a wall
Curtain	Fortified wall surrounding a castle
Enceinte	Enclosure; ward of a castle
Garderobe	Latrine
Hoard, Hoarding	Wooden gallery thrown out from the top of a wall or tower, so that the defenders could command the base and prevent attackers from mining or firing

Machicolation	Virtually a stone hoarding; an overhanging parapet with openings in its floor, through which an attack could be made on the assailants below
Meurtrière	Opening over the gate, enabling the defenders to drop stones on the attackers or, more frequently, to pour water on fires kindled in an attempt to burn the gate
Motte	Earthen mound of a Norman castle
Portcullis	Iron grating which could be raised or lowered in front of a gate or doorway
Postern	Back or side entrance
Ward	Courtyard or bailey of a castle
Yett	A Scottish form of the portcullis; a gate formed of intersecting iron bars, penetrating each other vertically and horizontally, the method of intersection being reversed in alternate panels. The yett could be even more formidable than the portcullis and was eventually banned, exceptions being made in the case of a few favoured nobles.

Printed in England by R. J. Acford Ltd., Chichester